Original title:
Where Pothos Roam

Copyright © 2025 Creative Arts Management OÜ
All rights reserved.

Author: Ethan Prescott
ISBN HARDBACK: 978-1-80581-793-2
ISBN PAPERBACK: 978-1-80581-320-0
ISBN EBOOK: 978-1-80581-793-2

Whispers in the Leafy Canopy

In the heights, the leaves conspire,
Chirping tales of a vine's desire.
One says, 'I slid on a butterfly!'
The others laugh, saying, 'No way to fly!'

With roots that tickle, branches that sway,
Lizards playing hide and seek all day.
Hushing whispers through the leafy spree,
'Did you see that lizard dance with glee?'

Stories Woven in Wild Tendrils

Tendrils spin their silly yarns,
Of squirrels wearing hats made of ferns.
One claims he saw a raccoon dress,
In a tuxedo, causing quite a mess!

The gossip spreads from leaf to leaf,
Of cheeky critters, and a comical thief.
'Where's my acorn?' the squirrel asks,
While birds just giggle, wearing their masks!

Nature's Silken Pathways

On trails of silk, the critters tread,
A snail wore shades, but lost his head.
The ants parade in tiny boots,
Strutting about in their fancy suits.

With every twist and leafy bend,
The mushrooms toast to a garden trend.
'Did you hear the one about the bee?'
'He tried to dance, but fell from the tree!'

Tangles of Light and Green

In the chaos of the jungle's hum,
The monkeys echo, 'Here we come!'
Swinging low, then soaring high,
'This vine's my swing, oh me, oh my!'

With jests and japes, the blossoms giggle,
'Watch that cat—he'll take a wiggle!'
As sunbeams dance on leaves so bright,
Nature's laughter echoes, pure delight!

Songs of the Untouched Path

Beneath the leaves, they sway and tease,
These vines have secrets, if you please.
With each small step along the way,
They giggle softly, 'Come and play!'

In sunlight's glow, they twist and twirl,
They beckon squirrels, and caterpillars whirl.
A dance of green, a vibrant show,
Get lost in laughter as they grow!

Frogs leap high with a silly croak,
Against the vines, they play the joke.
A catnap's chased by a buzzing bee,
Those untouched trails make all feel free!

So join the fun, embrace the cheer,
These verdant paths bring joy near.
With every twist and turn we find,
A chuckle shared, a heart unpinned.

The Climb of the Curious Heart

Bouncing blooms on a winding way,
Tickling toes, come out to play.
A twist of charm, a giggle bright,
Climbing on joy, reaching new height!

The vines are ropes in a leafy maze,
Where branches sway in a silly craze.
Each step's a chance to dance and sing,
With every heartbeat, let laughter spring!

Wobbling critters join the trail,
Their antics tell a funny tale.
With snorts and squeaks, they pave the way,
In nature's bounce, we frolic and play!

So grab a bud and take a chance,
Join the vines in a playful dance.
The curious heart can surely roam,
In leafy lanes, we find our home!

In the Embrace of Nature's Veil

Leaves gossip softly, swaying with cheer,
Mossy whispers tease, 'Come dance over here!'
Frogs wear tiny hats, croaking in style,
While squirrels hold meetings, gossiping a while.

Birds play charades, with their beaks in the air,
The wind carries laughter, a joke everywhere.
Bumblebees buzzing, in tune with the trees,
Nature's a circus, just do as you please.

The Trail of the Heartstrings

Worms in a conga line, wriggling with glee,
A snail says, 'Hurry up! You're slower than me!'
A beetle with shades rolls by on a beat,
While crickets provide the rhythm so sweet.

Twirling daisies dance, in the breeze they sway,
Each petal a dancer, brightening the day.
A butterfly prances, looking quite bold,
In this merry realm, the fun never gets old.

Dancing Shadows of the Forest

In the shadowy corners, the owls start to wink,
As foxes play tag, with a sly little wink.
Mice in tuxedos, hold a grand soirée,
Under the moon's gaze, they all shout hooray!

Trees drum their branches, in rhythmic delight,
While fireflies twinkle, lighting up the night.
A raccoon with style, sporting a bow,
Invites all critters to join in the show.

Through the Canopy's Embrace

Branches cradle secrets, like hats on a bed,
Each rustle a giggle, each gust sets the thread.
A moose trying yoga, lost all the grace,
But laugh we must, in this wild, funny space.

Monkeys trade rumors, swinging from high,
While turtles debate what the clouds look like,
As shadows hold court, sharing tales with delight,
In nature's embrace, every moment feels right.

Vines that Touch the Sky

In the garden, they stretch high,
Twisting happily, oh my!
They climb the fence and dance about,
Whispering secrets, without a doubt.

A squirrel stares, then jumps in fright,
As they wave hello, what a sight!
With leafy fingers, they paint the town,
Making each moment a merry crown.

They launch a race with the sun so bright,
Getting tangled in morning light.
Chasing shadows, they laugh and spin,
Playing games where the fun begins.

With every breeze, they gleefully sway,
Creating tunes that make the day
Turn into a whimsical cheer,
As if the sky had cast its beer.

A Symphony of Green Heartbeats

In the corner of the room they play,
Rustling leaves in a jazzy sway.
Each tendril a note in a leafy song,
Reminding us where we all belong.

The cacti giggle, the ferns do sway,
As if plants gather to have a buffet.
The orchids gossip with a nod and grin,
While the pothos join in, oh what a din!

Roots tap dance on the cool, soft soil,
As sunlight bathes them in life's rich foil.
They croon their tales of audacious fun,
Creating a choir, never to shun.

Close your eyes, let the sounds consume,
As leafy laughter fills the room.
In every heartbeat, a giggle thrives,
A symphony where only green survives.

Tales from the Verdant Corners

In a corner of the room so snug,
A tale unfolds with a playful tug.
The vines weave stories, thick and thin,
With every twist, a new win.

A leaf sighs, "Oh what a view,"
While another screams, "I'm stuck like glue!"
They tell of rain that danced on roofs,
And moonlit nights where they found their grooves.

The pots are laughing, what a sight,
As vines twist wrong, then get it right.
They play hide and seek with the light,
Crafting memories, such pure delight.

Grab a chair, come sit and stay,
And listen to the plants' splay.
For in this home of green and cheer,
Lies humor and joy that feels so near.

The Language of Climbing Hearts

There's a language spoken in leafy greens,
Of dreams and wishes, of playful scenes.
They twist and curl like a happy rhyme,
Mimicking the steeple of time.

With every climb, they whisper truths,
About silly frogs and playful sleuths.
Rattling pots in their joyful quest,
They share laughter at life's behest.

Each tendril watches the world unfold,
With giggles shared that will never grow old.
They chatter softly with roots as friends,
Creating a bond that never bends.

So let them climb, let them explore,
In every nook and leafy door.
For in their hearts, a glee so bright,
Turns the mundane into pure delight.

Roots that Speak to the Stars

In pots of clay, they wiggle tight,
All dreaming dreams of cosmic flight.
With every twist, a tale they weave,
Of grapes and moons and nights to believe.

They whisper low in leafy tones,
About the dreams of ancient stones.
With roots that search through soil and skies,
They plant a wink in nature's eyes.

As sunshine hugs their leafy crowns,
They giggle softly, dance in towns.
Tangled tales in twisted vines,
They work on jokes and silly lines.

So here's a toast to roots so bold,
In planty jokes, their wisdom's gold.
With every sprout, in laughter grow,
They share the joy that only they know.

Ferns and Fantasies

In shady spots where wild ferns dance,
They spin around in a green romance.
With fronds that wave as if to cheer,
They tell of fantasies that draw us near.

Whispers float on the gentle breeze,
Of secret worlds among the trees.
Each frond a tale, a quirky jest,
It's nature's way to entertain the best.

They gather round for nightly talks,
About the dreams of garden walks.
With every leaf a story's thread,
In laughter, plant-life's joy is spread.

In the moonlight's glow, they start to scheme,
Of wild adventures, and things to dream.
Ferns with giggles that never cease,
In the garden of fantasies, they find their peace.

The Wanderlust of Greenery

Green things packed in a travel bag,
With dreams of places and a tiny rag.
From jungles thick to deserts bare,
They plot their routes with leafy flair.

A cactus plans a trip to town,
While ivies map the backroads down.
With pulpy hearts and jovial cheer,
No hop is too far for greenery here.

Bamboo poles with tales so tall,
They share their plans at every call.
In cozy pots, they scheme and dream,
A wanderlust the world can't deem.

So let's not bind these leaves so free,
For every journey's laughter's key.
In sunny spots or shadowed gloom,
They'll roam the earth, dispelling gloom.

When Life Finds a Way

In cracks and crevices, green things sprout,
Life's cheeky wink, a hoot, a shout.
With every crack, they claim their stay,
A testament, when life finds a way.

Little buds in the pavement's seam,
Proving nature's rich, enduring dream.
With roots like giggles, they spread wide,
In every corner, they take pride.

Through storms and sun, they bend but don't break,
Their funny faces, what a mistake!
Resilient greens, they dance and sway,
A joyful reminder, come what may.

So next time you see a plant so bold,
Remember the stories that they hold.
When laughter's found in every sway,
You'll know it's true when life finds a way.

When Leaves Tell Secret Stories

In the garden, leaves do chatter,
Whisper tales, like birds that flatter.
One says, 'I've danced with the breeze!'
Another claims, 'I've tickled bees!'

They gossip about the sun's warm rays,
And giggle at the clouds' odd ways.
'Look at us, we're green and spry!'
'We really do know how to fly!'

Funky patterns on each green face,
Remind us of our leafy grace.
In every rustle, in every twirl,
They spread their laughter across the world.

Nourishing the Climb

Up, up, the vines do creep,
With dreams that make the gardener leap.
'I'm taller than the fence!' one shouts,
While nearby cacti roll their spouts.

One leaf waves at a wandering bee,
'Come join my feast, just wait and see!'
Not all get along, but that's just fine,
The more, the merrier, in this viney line!

Curled up ferns join the party late,
Spreading joy, they celebrate fate.
In the tussle of leaves and shoots,
Are laughter and love in fuzzy roots.

Entwined Hearts of Nature

A twist and tangle, these plants do play,
With hearts entwined in a green ballet.
One plant giggles, 'I'm your best bet!'
'Nope,' says the flower, 'I'm not done yet!'

In the moonlight, their shadows sway,
Whispering secrets of night and day.
Petals prance, while stems stand tall,
Nature's comedy, a blooming ball!

'You think you're funny?' a fern does tease,
'Try to keep up with my breezy squeeze!'
With rivals turned friends, they dance and spin,
Nature's jesters, through thick and thin.

The Velvet Path of Graceful Growth

On a soft path, the leaves do stroll,
With velvety dreams, they've set a goal.
'Where will we end?' one leaf does ask,
'At the sun's door, that's our task!'

With plucky roots, they giggle loud,
Sipping dew like a leafy crowd.
Every bump and twist a dance,
Nature's fun, given half a chance!

A rabbit hops and joins the fun,
Laughing as he races, no tree to shun.
'Together we grow, side by side,'
In this velvet path, we take great pride!

Growing Among the Forgotten

In the corner of the room, they bloom,
Silent mischief, filling the gloom.
Green little champs with leaves so wide,
Telling secrets, with nowhere to hide.

Dust bunnies dance as they share a joke,
While sunlight beams, the shadows poke.
A sip of water, a hearty cheer,
What a party, with no one here!

They climb the wall, like cats on a spree,
Stretching their limbs, looking fancy-free.
With pot in hand, it's quite the sight,
Planting dreams under the moonlight.

Amidst the chaos, they claim their throne,
Swaying with laughter on leaves overgrown.
Who knew the potted could party so grand?
In their green kingdom, they make the stand!

Dreams in Every Leaf

On the window sill, the greenery plays,
Counting the minutes, counting the days.
With roots deep down and dreams so high,
They plot their take-off, aiming for the sky.

The sunlight flicks like an old movie reel,
While leaves whisper tales they can almost feel.
"Dance with the wind!" they say with a laugh,
As a breeze strolls through—nature's photograph.

In every vein, there's a wild ballet,
With wormy waltzes, they wiggle and sway.
Each leaf a canvas, in shades so divine,
Crafting funny stories in nature's design.

A hint of mischief in every green plume,
With jokes tucked away, they lighten the room.
Growing in silence, but bursting with cheer,
In botanical dreams, they've no need for fear!

Bridges of Nature's Whisper

In the wildest corners, adventures await,
Nature's teen rebels, refusing debate.
Swinging like monkeys, those tendrilled vines,
Creating a party where sunlight aligns.

With soil-stained hands, they build their nests,
In crooked pots, it's a verdant fest.
They giggle and shimmer, inviting the sun,
"Come join our fiesta! Oh, this will be fun!"

A dance on the table, a twist on the chair,
With every new bloom, there's humor to share.
Nature's own bridge, with laughter entwined,
In the land of the leafy, joy is defined.

Petals in whispers and branches that sway,
Conspire with breezes, in perfect ballet.
They plot and they scheme as they bask in their fame,
Nature's whispers giggle—oh, what a game!

Echoed in the Canopy

Up high in the branches where the sparrows fly,
The leaves gossip stories as shadows drift by.
"Did you hear about Freddie? He bloomed just last week,"
All the plants giggled, it's fun to critique.

Across the great sky, laughter's let loose,
In a world of green giggles, a welcome excuse.
Swinging like pendulums, hanging in flair,
They jive with the breezes that tickle the air.

Echoing joy with roots locked tight,
They stretch and they bend, catching the light.
Each leaf a dancer in nature's parade,
Spreading the laughter where dreams gently fade.

With petals for pillows, they rest for a while,
While raindrops drum softly, they bask in the smile.
In forests of folly, under skies so grand,
Life blooms in the humor that nature has planned.

A Dappled Path to Serenity

On a path dappled with sun,
Silly squirrels had a run,
Sneaking nuts, one by one,
Laughing in the warm, bright fun.

The whistling breeze plays tricks,
With leafy whispers, it kicks,
A toad jumps, a dance, a mix,
Nature's humor in the fix.

Bouncing blooms join the chase,
A butterfly joins the race,
Wearing colors with pure grace,
In this joyful, silly space.

Time stumbles, loses track,
As creatures gather, no lack,
In dappled light, no need to pack,
Together, let's enjoy the snack.

Romantic Interludes in Leafy Arbors

In leafy shades, a kiss so sweet,
Two frogs hop, then skip their feet,
Mismatched like a clumsy beat,
Nature laughs, a fun retreat.

A bushy tail swipes through the air,
With acorns flying everywhere,
Lovebirds giggle, unaware,
They snuggle up, without a care.

The vines entwine in playful glee,
Creating shades for you and me,
While a grumpy old bee, you see,
Buzzes gruffly, 'Let me be!'

Underneath the leafy dome,
Hearts find laughter, never home,
In romance, we can freely roam,
Nature's jest, our love, our poem.

Clinging to Dreams and Time

On a branch, a dream takes flight,
An old squirrel, oh what a sight,
Clings to time with all his might,
Hoarding nuts, a comical plight.

The clouds nap, a lazy crew,
While daydreams chase, as they do,
Bumbling owls in a huddle too,
Whisper secrets, just a few.

A frisky breeze starts a tease,
Playing tag among the trees,
Chasing shadows, with such ease,
Life's a giggle, such a breeze.

So let us cling to dreams and cheer,
With silly friends always near,
Each moment filled with laughter clear,
In this garden, let's persevere.

Festivities Among Green Shadows

Green shadows dance under the light,
With nightly critters, such delight,
An owl croons a tune so tight,
As fireflies twinkle, sparkling bright.

Gathered friends all in a ring,
Beetles play drums, what a thing!
While chipmunks in tuxedos sing,
The forest echoes, let joy spring.

Laughter bubbles, the notes take flight,
A caterpillar waltzes, what a sight,
Beneath the moon, what a night,
Joyful ruckus, pure delight.

In this festive, leafy patch,
With every sound, the moments match,
Nature's hearts, a perfect catch,
In green shadows, laughter's hatch.

Echoes of Silence Among the Leaves

In the garden, whispers play,
Leaves giggle in a sunlit sway.
A squirrel dances, chasing its tail,
While birds critique from their leafy hail.

The breeze tickles the stems so fine,
As shadows begin to intertwine.
'What's that noise?' the fern demands,
An echo of laughter from leafy bands.

Twilight's Embrace of Verdant Joy

Under stars, the plants convene,
Sharing secrets, goofy and keen.
A cactus jokes about his prickle,
While vines sway, doing a quick tickle.

The daisies laugh, a petal joke,
As crickets join, their chorus awoke.
'Twilight's here!' the tulips cheer loud,
While night wraps all in a leafy shroud.

Rhapsody in Green Tones

Each leaf plays a note, so bright,
Creating melodies in pale moonlight.
A dandelion sings, 'I'm pure and free!'
While ferns respond, 'Just ask the bee.'

A plant parade marches through the night,
With stomping roots, oh what a sight!
Berry bushes dance, colorful and bold,
In this green symphony, laughter unfolds.

A Journey Through Leafy Labyrinths

With every twist, a new delight,
The plants conspire, plotting for light.
A rogue vine, in mischief, sways,
Tripping the feet of lost bees in a haze.

Chasing shadows in leafy lanes,
While laughter tumbles—who's got the reins?
'Can I borrow your sunshine?' a rogue plant asks,
Yet only finds the ferns in their masks.

Nature's Tender Embrace of Resilience

In the garden, plants make a fuss,
With leaves that dance and roots that discuss.
A flower sneezes, petals fly,
A bumblebee hums, oh my oh my!

The sun shines bright, but rain's on the way,
A squirrel sprints by, trying to play.
The daisies giggle, they twist and sway,
While thorns and brambles start to weigh.

Lively greens stretch high, a playful bunch,
They poke at the clouds, their favorite lunch.
"Hey, don't hog the sky!" the daisies shout,
While the chill winds blow, they laugh and pout.

Nature's antics, a circus so grand,
With nature's humor, it's all so planned.
The vines tease the trees, daring them to dance,
In this quirky place, all take a chance.

Tendrils of Solitude

In a quiet nook, the tendrils creep,
Whispering secrets while others sleep.
A lizard sunbathes with a cheeky grin,
'Hope I don't sunburn, it's quite a sin!'

They twist and tangle, play peek-a-boo,
Hiding from spiders, who wish they'd skew.
The solitary leaf, a contemplative chap,
Wonders if solitude's just a trap.

The moonlight chuckles at vines' late-night woes,
As they argue with shadows about where to grow.
While a witty worm curls up on the lane,
"Might as well dance in this drops of rain!"

As the stars wink above, with mischief in mind,
The tendrils invent stories, one of a kind.
In solitude's comfort, they find their own song,
In the wild, tangled embrace where they belong.

In the Shade of Green Whispers

Under the leaves, whispers float by,
'Did you see the cat? She's such a sly!'
The grass giggles at a worm's funny hat,
While daisies debate if they're all that.

The squirrels tell stories of nuts that they've hid,
While ferns giggle softly, "Just look at that kid!"
The breeze gets the joke, and tickles the trees,
As the petals chuckle, not wanting to freeze.

Each rustle and ruffle adds to the fun,
'Maybe we'll grow more under this sun!'
While a playful breeze brings leaves to delight,
The mushrooms just laugh, 'Hey, we're quite right!'

In the shade of green, laughter is rife,
Nature's design is a comical life.
The quirks of the forest, a whimsical spree,
In whispers of green, all are carefree.

Vines that Touch the Sky

The eager vines stretch, scratching the sky,
"I'll touch that cloud!" says one with a sigh.
While others just giggle, 'You've lost your mind,
Can't you see how the winds are unkind?'

They twist and they twirl, a circus in green,
Waving their arms like they've never been seen.
A ladybug sighs, 'What's all this fuss?'
While climbing the letters in nature's big bus!

The sun joins the party, shines down with glee,
As the vines tell the tales of the bugs they see.
'You think you're so tall?' chirps a tiny sprout,
'But I've got some dreams that will knock you out!'

With laughter and light, this gathering grows,
In a leafy embrace, life merrily flows.
The vines keep on reaching, with joy in their heart,
In this funny little world, each plays their part.

Gratitude in Every Leafy Layer

In every twist of green we find,
A gratitude that's intertwined.
Leaves whisper secrets to the air,
Thanking sunlight everywhere.

With every droplet from the sky,
Plants do a dance, oh my, oh my!
Roots are giggling in the dirt,
Tickling worms, in playful flirt.

Branches stretch like arms so wide,
Sharing joy, with every stride.
Petals blush, they can't contain,
Their laughter in a gentle rain.

So here's a toast to leafy friends,
Where gratitude never ends.
In every garden, great or small,
Nature's humor, we're part of it all.

Dancing through the Garden's Breath

The daisies sway, they smile and twirl,
As bees come buzzing, give us a whirl.
Butterflies flutter with a comical glide,
In the breezy waltz, they take great pride.

Silly worms in soil dive low,
Trading jokes down under, oh what a show!
Leaves rustle with laughter, a chorus delight,
In this festive garden, all is just right.

A single raindrop splashes with glee,
"What a ride," they laugh, "just wait and see!"
Sunflowers nodding, bold and bright,
Waving their heads in pure delight.

So let's embrace the joyous sway,
Join the dance beneath the day.
In every petal, every breeze,
There's fun to be found, if you please!

Portraits of Growth in Hidden Spaces

In shadowed nooks, the sprouts emerge,
Tiny giants, beginning to surge.
They stretch and reach, with playful might,
A barometer of joy in the night.

Cracks in pavement hold secrets tight,
In their stubbornness, they find the light.
Silly vines make their bold ascent,
Over fences, their time is spent.

Rooftops play host to a leafy parade,
Every inch a game, never delayed.
With smiles that loom, causes for cheer,
The more they grow, the less fear.

So let's seek out the quirky greens,
In hidden places, hear their dreams.
For life's a canvas, in every trace,
A portrait of joy, in every space.

Vines that Write Their Own Stories

Vines curl out like a scribbler's hand,
Sketching tales across the land.
In twists and turns, they weave a plot,
Humor tangled in every knot.

Their leaves are pages laughing so bright,
Sharing adventures, a comical rite.
Climbing walls with style and flair,
Each climb a giggle, when they dare.

With a wink they tickle the sky,
"Let's see how high we can simply fly!"
Roots underground whisper tales with glee,
In the underground, humor runs free.

So as they stretch and reach to write,
Let's join their stories, with pure delight.
In the tangled web of leafy delight,
There's laughter aplenty, shining bright.

Rooted Yet Free

In the corner, a plant takes flight,
With leaves so bold, they dance in the light.
Stuck in a pot, yet dreaming of skies,
Whispers of freedom in earthy guise.

Neighbors stare, as it sways with glee,
Imagining trips to the land of the free.
"Where's my passport?" the pothos would plead,
Tangled in roots, yet longing for speed.

Reaching for sun, it giggles in green,
In this house, it's the brightest it's been.
With every shake, it shouts, "Look at me!"
A vine with a vision, oh so carefree!

So here it stays, with a wild little grin,
Dancing around in a pot made of tin.
Rooted yet free, it laughs with delight,
A comedy show in the warm morning light.

Portraits of Life in Color

With colors so bright, they paint the room,
Leaves like artists, they break from the gloom.
The pot's a gallery, the sun a muse,
Each new sprout shares a story to choose.

Crimson and green in a humorous clash,
As if they're all ready for a joyous bash.
"Bring on the sunlight, let's soak up the fun!"
They giggle and wiggle—oh what a run!

Laughter erupts in the tangles of vines,
Painting the air with the best of designs.
Tea parties happen on the window ledge,
While leaves share their dreams with a leafy pledge.

So take a good look, at this colorful show,
Where portraits of life in bloom brightly glow.
Each leaf a slapstick, each stem a new tale,
In the garden of humor, our laughter prevails.

Ascending Through Light and Shadow

In sunbeam scripts and shadows below,
A plant climbs high, putting on a show.
With every twist, it giggles aloud,
"Look at my height, I'm tall and so proud!"

Dancing through darkness, it searches for light,
Swaying with joy, oh what a sight!
"Catch me if you can!" it teases the breeze,
Like a nursery rhyme, it does as it pleases.

Up towards the ceiling, it reaches for fame,
In this leafy race, there's no need for shame.
Fumbling and tumbling, but never in dread,
For a laugh is the treasure that lies just ahead.

As branches grow higher, stories unfold,
Of adventures in sunlight, both witty and bold.
Ascending through currents of shadow and shine,
An acrobat of green, so perfectly fine.

The Botanical Ballet of Nature

Leaves pirouette in a whimsical waltz,
A ballet of green with no need for faults.
"Two hops to the left, and spin like a top!"
The room bursts with laughter, now they can't stop.

In pots they embrace, a choreographed scene,
With roots intertwined, they dance so serene.
"Watch my grand leap!" one shouts, full of cheer,
While another just giggles, "I'm stuck over here!"

A twist and a turn, oh how they sway,
Nature's own show, come watch every day.
Each leaf a performer, each stem takes the stage,
In this botanical ballet, wisdom and age.

So gather around for this verdant delight,
As branches all fumble, yet sparkle so bright.
In the theater of growth, laughter reigns free,
The twirling of nature is a sight to see!

Emerald Vines in Dappled Light

In a tangle of green, who knows what's found?
A reptile, a squirrel, all tumbling around.
The leaves make a party, they sway and they groove,
While birds do their dance, they really can move!

Sunbeams tickle petals, giggles in the air,
As a gnome takes a selfie, with vines in his hair.
The shadows play tricks, like a game of charades,
While nature's comedians pull off their escapades.

Frogs leap in, laughing, on a lily pad stage,
With each ribbit, they're sharing their latest page.
A chatty old snail, in his shell, takes a seat,
Exclaims, "This is better than the last Sunday feast!"

So join all the critters in this leafy delight,
As emerald vines twirl, bringing joy to the night.
With every green gesture, nature's humor thrives,
In the jungle of laughter, oh, how the fun dives!

Lush Whisper of the Green

In the lushness beyond where the green fingers brush,
Hedgehogs wear hats, and the rabbits all hush.
A breeze carries laughter, tickling the leaves,
As butterflies gossip, weaving jokes like thieves.

A curious lizard claims he can dance,
While a frog in the pond thinks he's got a great chance.
They twirl and they twist, in a funny display,
As mushrooms keep score, in a fungi ballet.

Squirrels devise plans for a nutty parade,
While vines drop confetti, joining the charade.
The sun giggles softly, its rays in a swirl,
As the whole forest revels, the leaves start to twirl.

In this whispering green where the laughter hangs low,
Nature's humor is boundless, the joy always grows.
A symphony played by the critters so spry,
In a land of delight, as the laughter floats by!

Tendrils of Tranquility

Among the curling tendrils, there's mischief at play,
A sloth with a grin asks, "Can I stay for the day?"
While raccoons debate who's the funniest chap,
A deer rolls his eyes, and takes a long nap.

The ivy entwines with the tales of the past,
Each leaf holding secrets that giggle and last.
A rabbit, quite dapper, in glasses so bright,
Claims wisdom in jazz, as the moon starts the night.

Figments of laughter pop up all around,
As squirrels in top hats march with flair, grace unbound.
They pirouette in circles, as laughter does loom,
Celebrating the quirks that bloom in the gloom.

With tendrils embracing, they dance through the green,
In their world of fun, where the joy is unseen.
So come take a stroll, where the smiles are wide,
In this tranquil jungle, with good humor as guide!

In the Shadow of Climbing Dreams

Beneath the sprawling vines, the antics unfold,
With critters on stages, their stories retold.
A gopher with maracas shakes them with flair,
While a cat plays the drums, serenading the air.

In shadows of dreams that stretch towards the sky,
Reptiles recite rhymes, with a wink in their eye.
A turtle, so clever, spins tales from his shell,
Of mischief and mayhem, all splendid to tell.

The hummingbirds giggle, over flowers they dart,
As a wise old owl muses, "Is that an art?"
Nature's little theater, with laughter it glows,
In the tapestry woven where silliness flows.

So venture where dreams intertwine with the green,
In shadows and sunlight, let humor convene.
For climbing the tales is the best kind of climb,
In this leafy domain where the punchlines are prime!

Harmonies of Nature's Embrace

Underneath the leafy spread,
Squirrels throw a ball instead.
Birds sing tunes in snappy beats,
Flower beds hold comedic feats.

Nature's laughter fills the air,
A frog jumps high without a care.
Worms do the cha-cha on the ground,
While ants march in a silly sound.

Bees play tag with buzzing zest,
They zig and zag; it's quite the fest!
Laughter echoes, soft and sweet,
In this green space, fun's complete.

With every twist, each shrub and vine,
Nature's joke is pure divine.
Life's a dance, a shiny show,
Come join the fun where rivers flow!

Growth in the Unseen Corners

In cracks where no one dares to peek,
Mischief blooms, it's rather cheek!
Tiny sprouts and weeds galore,
Unexpected joy at every door.

Caterpillars wear silly hats,
While ladybugs chit-chat with bats.
Each shadow hides a playful plot,
Nature's jesters like it hot!

Roots stretch out in zany ways,
They tickle toes on sunny days.
Grow a mustache, wear a grin,
In secret spots, the fun begins.

Watch it all, the wild parade,
In quiet corners, plans are laid.
The unseen jokes are bright and bold,
In funny shades of green and gold!

The Art of Green Archways

Through arches made of vines and leaves,
Chuckle at the webs they weave.
Giggling flowers wave hello,
As breezes join their garden show.

Lizards bask on sunny stones,
With silly poses, striking tones.
Butterflies flap with flair so bright,
Making art in joyful flight.

Beneath the bows, secrets spread,
Singing songs no one has read.
Laughter dances on the breeze,
While daisies giggle with such ease.

Nature's canvas bursts alive,
Where whimsical thoughts can thrive.
In green archways, laughter reigns,
Each turn brings joy, no room for pains!

Wandering Through Life's Verdant Maze

In a maze of green we roam,
Confused, we laugh, not far from home.
Twisting paths play peek-a-boo,
Every turn reveals something new.

Curly fronds with laughs so sly,
Tickle toes that wander by.
Flowers wink with sunny cheer,
Joining in the silly sphere.

A hedgehog giggles, a fern takes flight,
It's a quirky show from day to night.
With every step, a funny scene,
In this lively, leafy green.

Life's a maze, so let's not stress,
It's meant for laughter, fun, and jest.
So wander forth, enjoy the craze,
In this merry, verdant maze!

The Language of Leaves

In the forest, leaves conspire,
Whispering secrets like a choir.
One said, 'I'm feeling quite green,'
The others laughed, 'You're a real scene!'

Each rustle tells a quirky tale,
Of raccoons dreaming on a rail.
They wear top hats made of bark,
While squirrels dance, they leave their mark.

A breeze passes, leaves all shiver,
'Did you see that? I couldn't quiver!'
They giggle then in playful glee,
As shadows move, a leafy spree!

So next time you stroll through the green,
Listen close, join their unseen scene.
For in the trees, a laughter blooms,
Among the roots, in leafy rooms.

A Journey through Tangled Dreams

Through tangled paths of leafy lore,
I found a snail, his name is Thor.
He wore a shell, shiny and bright,
Said, 'Hop on quick, let's take flight!'

We soared above the ferns so tall,
Past mushrooms that grinned with a sprawl.
Each flower winked, a colorful tease,
As we sped through the playful breeze.

'Careful!' cried a dandelion sprout,
'Don't crash down, this dream's too stout!'
But Thor just giggled, 'I've got style,'
With every twist, he flashed a smile.

So here we go, through winks and dreams,
In this lush life, nothing's as it seems.
A journey filled with laughter's song,
In leafy realms, we both belong!

Echoes of the Lush

In the lush, where the wild things meet,
A chorus sings, oh so sweet!
A frog in boots stole my first glance,
Said, 'Join my band, let's start a dance!'

Beetles play drums on hollow logs,
While fireflies twinkle, like starlit frogs.
'Dance with us,' they call with glee,
In a bounce full of verdant spree!

The grass tickles, a jolly tune,
As we leap beneath the laughing moon.
Each critter sways, a happy sway,
In the lush, we dance 'til the day!

So if you're down, just take a chance,
Join the froggy, leafy dance.
For in this echo, joy takes flight,
In the heart of the green delight!

Secrets of the Climbing Heart

A vine once whispered, 'I'm quite the catch,'
With twists and turns, a climbing sketch.
She'd scale the trellis with such flair,
Said, 'Love's a climb, but I'll get there!'

Up she went, in leafy grace,
While birds cheered loud, oh what a race!
'If I fall, I'll bounce like a pro!'
The branches laughed, 'We'll never let go!'

But mid-climb, she found a rogue bee,
Doing the tango, so wild and free.
'Join me!' he buzzed with a cheeky grin,
So they twirled round, let the dance begin!

In the end, they reached the top,
With petals bloomed, they'd never stop.
For love's a climb full of cheer,
In every twist, we hold it dear!

The Essence of Verdant Journeys

In jungles deep, the vines take flight,
They twirl and leap with sheer delight.
A banana peel, oh what a sight,
Nature's slip-and-slide, what pure delight!

Silly snails in a rubbery race,
They slide right past with a funny face.
The flowers giggle in their own space,
As petals tickle and soft winds chase.

Lush fronds wave like fans at a show,
As butterflies dance with a vibrant glow.
Each plant grins wide, joining the flow,
In a leafy carnival, don't you know?

Among the greens, a spider spins art,
Its web's a puzzle, a twisted part.
In photosynthesis, plants break hearts,
With jokes so punny, who needs smart carts?

Shades of Green in the Twilight Hour

The twilight whispers, colors collide,
In shades of green, the oddities hide.
A frog in a tux, ready to bide,
While a squirrel debates, 'Should I slide?'

The moonlit leaves start the party glow,
And little beetles dance, toe to toe.
With jellybean skies, oh what a show,
To laugh at the leaves in the breezy flow.

A raccoon giggles with paws all shiny,
Stealing snacks—oh, thoughts so whiny!
In this dark, every creature looks tiny,
Yet their humor shines, always so briny!

As crickets chirp their goofy tunes,
The fireflies flicker like shiny balloons.
In the shades of green, where magic strews,
Life's a silly dance beneath the moons!

Pursuit of Light in a Leafy World

In leafy realms, the sunbeams chase,
Plants reach for light, in their sunny race.
A rogue fern makes a curious face,
While vines plot mischief at a rapid pace.

The shadows creep, but the laughter grows,
As flowers gossip, what everyone knows.
With winks and giggles, oh how it shows,
That even greens need fun to propose!

A chubby caterpillar with stripes so wide,
Dreams of a snack with each leisurely stride.
As stems sway gently, snickers collide,
In this leafy realm, giggles can't hide.

With every bloom, there's humor to find,
Nature cracks jokes, so cleverly designed.
In pursuit of light, they're all intertwined,
In a leafy world, where joy's the bind!

Enchanted Clusters Beneath the Sun

Beneath bright skies, where mischief gleams,
Clusters gather with funny dreams.
A pepper that giggles, bursting at seams,
And radishes roll, or so it seems!

As daisies whisper their jokes in jest,
The strawberries snicker, the very best.
A tomato grins, oh what a fest,
In a garden giggle, no moment's a rest!

The sunflower bows, with a hat on their head,
While the worms below are just laughing instead.
With each cheeky bloom, humor is spread,
In enchanted clusters, where jokes are fed!

With dancing clouds, and sunbeam cheers,
The plants tell tales that bring hearty jeers.
In this sunny realm, let's gather our peers,
To laugh with the greens throughout the years!

Climbing Through the Garden of Time

In a garden filled with whimsy,
Plants wear hats so bright and clingy.
The daisies giggle, tulips dance,
Sunlight gives every leaf a chance.

Ladder made of twigs and dreams,
Up we climb, or so it seems.
The time flies by, like bees in flight,
Tick-tock laughter, oh what a sight!

Squirrels competing in a race,
Chasing shadows, quickening pace.
Each vine is just a friend to hug,
Nature's charm, a warm, cozy rug.

Beneath the moon, the garden dips,
With wiggly worms and silly quips.
Time's a jester, ever so spry,
Waving goodbye as we climb high!

Nature's Graceful Ascension

A leaf in tights and roots with flair,
Sliding down a slippery stair.
The branches cheer, they rise and sing,
As nature dons its finest bling.

Clouds play hopscotch in the blue,
Roots giggle, saying, 'Look at you!'
Frogs wear crowns, the crickets hum,
In this garden, all is fun!

Climbing high on a vine-spiral,
Bananas shout, 'Join our trial!'
Every bloom has jokes to share,
With bees and bugs, all in the air.

In the branches of tomorrow's cheer,
Laughter grows, it's always near.
Nature's trickery, oh so grand,
In this place, we all can stand!

Echoes of Growth in Airy Spaces

In a patch of green, beneath the sun,
Flowers giggle, having fun.
The breezes whisper with a laugh,
As vines twine tight like a silly craft.

Echoes bounce from tree to tree,
Each laugh a note, so wild and free.
Shy bushes blush, then stand so tall,
While tiny mushrooms take the call.

Against the sky, the colors cheer,
From purple peas to bright green spheres.
Each sprout a joke, each root a tale,
Join the dance, let laughter sail.

Amidst the echoes, the joy is clear,
In every petal, life draws near.
A motley crew, this garden's glee,
Sings a tune of unity!

The Heart's Climbing Path

With a skip, the hearts entwine,
On winding trails where laughter shines.
Each step we take, a silly dance,
As nature joins in, a bright romance.

The bumblebees play hide-and-seek,
While tiny ants march, bold yet meek.
Together in this garden of jest,
We climb the path, we are so blessed!

Giggles bubble from the creek,
Nature's secrets, oh so cheek!
A snake in shades takes a stroll,
Winking with every tiny poll.

Roses tease with fragrance sweet,
While daisies prance on tiny feet.
In this heart-filled, climbing path,
We'll find our joy, escape the math!

Harmony Blossoms in Vined Arches

In twisting green, the laughter sprawls,
A vine's embrace, it playfully calls.
Leaves tickle feet in a game so grand,
Spinning in circles, the garden's band.

With each bright bloom, surprises sprout,
A floral joke that leaves us in doubt.
Who knew a plant could dance and tease?
Nature's jesters among the trees!

Vines swing low like giddy kids,
Hiding secrets like playful bids.
In every nook a story's spun,
A floral romp, having some fun!

So let the petals guide our glee,
In tangled laughter, wild and free.
With every step, new tales are found,
In vined arches, joy abounds!

Tales of the Climbing Wild

In every twist, a yarn unfolds,
Of leafy mischief, brave and bold.
A lizard laughs, a bee hums low,
Tales of the wild, put on a show.

The vines declare a charming coup,
Wrapping trees in a leafy stew.
With snickers soft from flowers bright,
Nature giggles deep into the night.

Oh, how the ivy loves to sway,
Like it's auditioning for Broadway!
Each curl and climb a comic stride,
In the great green world, joy can't hide.

From tiny buds to sprawling leaves,
They weave a plot that never leaves.
With each new twist, let laughter grow,
In the climbing wild, let good times flow!

The Artistry of Nature's Twists

With swirling greens and vibrant hues,
Nature's art, one cannot refuse.
A montage of fun in every curl,
As flowers frolic and petals swirl.

The twine of nature, a clever prank,
Vines make mischief, as they flank.
With giggles shared and whispers light,
Every leaf joins in the delight.

Like Jackson Pollock, splashes bright,
Nature's canvas in pure sunlight.
Each vine a brushstroke, bold and funny,
Painting the world in shades of honey.

So come and wander through this spree,
Where laughter grows on every tree.
In this artistry, we'll find our bliss,
In nature's twists, nothing is amiss!

A Lush Odyssey Under Sunlit Canopies

Beneath the boughs, where shadows play,
A vibrant carpet invites to stay.
Laughter echoes as we drift and glide,
In nature's fold, let joy reside.

The leaves above share playful glances,
While sunlight beckons for sweet dances.
A grasshopper hops, a regal knight,
In this realm where the world feels right.

Every rustle brings a cheeky grin,
As buzzing bees let the fun begin.
With giggles as loud as a lion's roar,
Nature teases, always wanting more!

So come explore this leafy maze,
Where joy is found in wild displays.
Under the canopies, let spirits fly,
In this lush journey, we'll touch the sky!

Embracing Earth's Vertical Canvas

In a jungle of green, a secret parade,
Vines doing the tango, in sunlight they wade.
Leaves flapping like flags on a breeze-borne spree,
Nature's silly dance, come join and be free.

Climbing the walls, they giggle and sway,
Photosynthesis giggles, come join in the play.
A lizard tap-dances on a mossy old log,
While frogs croak their tune to a happily weird frog.

From pot to pot, they all vie for a throne,
Sweeping the floor, they declare they've grown!
The garden's lush laughter dances on air,
As pot-holed mischief fills this wild lair.

Gazing up high, the climbers connect,
Nature's graffiti, what do you expect?
With every bright leaf, a giggle does bloom,
Embracing the canvas, they lighten the room.

Secrets Hidden in Leafy Shadows

Underneath the leaves, a committee of bugs,
Debating their plans, filled with mischievous hugs.
They giggle and whisper, in circles they plot,
What's next on their list? A sunny hot spot!

A bright little snail, with intentions so grand,
Moved slowly along, surveying the land.
"Let's travel up high for a holistic view,
Or nap 'neath this leaf, it's better for two!"

The ferns act aloof, with a side-eye so sly,
While orchids roll their petals, oh my, oh my!
"Join us dear friends, let's start a grand scheme,
To nap and eat snacks 'til dawn's early beam!"

Between blushing petals, the whispers abound,
Secrets they keep, in cool shadows found.
With laughter they thrive, in their leafy domain,
What mischief will bloom after this little rain?

The Serenity of Nature's Twists

Bending and twisting in a playful show,
The vines weave tales, in sunlight's warm glow.
Daring to dance, they giggle and sway,
Making fun of the clouds that float their way.

A squirrel in mid-leap, a branch's embrace,
Mistakenly crashed, at a rather brisk pace.
With a fluff of the tail, and a hasty retreat,
He declares it a win, in this comedic feat.

Moss hugs the stones in a soft, squishy hug,
While mushrooms tease roots, with a giggling shrug.
"Let's throw a wild party, under the stars!
With rhythms and dances, we'll shake all our jars!"

While gusts of wind play, in a whimsical waltz,
Nature's own chorus never halts.
In the whimsical twists, laughter winds tight,
Serenity blooms in a comical light.

When Green Dreams Take Flight

With roots in the dirt and heads in the sun,
The leaves stretch wide, clearly having some fun!
A breeze sends whispers of whimsical cheer,
As green dreams take flight, in the bark's gentle sphere.

Busy little seedlings with stories to tell,
Plot out their journeys, oh so very well.
"Let's grow up this way, and wiggle like mad,
Or down to that puddle, it's not all that bad!"

A daring old sprout took a leap of faith,
To dance with a butterfly, however brief.
They spun and they twirled, what a sight to behold,
Two playful companions, daring and bold!

The clouds chuckled low, making shadows that tease,
As laughter echoed through the rustling leaves.
When dreams take to flight, in garden's embrace,
Every vine echoes joy, in their leafy space.

Veins of the Wild

In the jungle of my hall,
Vines decide to have a brawl.
They tangle up my chair and desk,
It's a wild plant masquerade desk!

Creeping high, they climb the wall,
Shouting vines, they have a ball.
I can't find my books or shoes,
All thanks to leafy avocause!

Each leaf is laughing, what a sight,
Swinging 'round in sheer delight.
I swear I heard them whisper 'hey',
As I tripped and fell today!

A jungle in my humble room,
With greenery that dares to bloom.
Next time I'll ignore the bright,
Just to avoid this leafy plight!

Portraits of a Climbing Soul

In the corner where they dare,
Plants are wrangling without care.
A drama queen with slinky green,
My living room's an art scene!

They strike poses full of sass,
Waving leaves, they've got class.
I swear they wink and giggle loud,
Unbothered by a frowning crowd!

A vine in the window, a true star,
Swaying idly, like a rock guitar.
As I pass, I hear them cheer,
"Another round, shout-out, my dear!"

Art on the walls? Nah, just the greens,
In this gallery of giggles and beans.
They climb higher, reaching for fame,
My sneaky friends, what a wild game!

Chronicles of the Cascading Green

Once upon a table high,
Foliage started to fly.
With a twist, oh what a dance,
Threw my papers in a trance!

"Oh help!" I called, "Keep it tame!"
But the leaves just laughed in fame.
They donned hats, a wild fest,
Pothos party! Who'd have guessed?

They flicked their leaves in pure surprise,
Dancing vines, the hearty spies.
With each sway and every twirl,
My quiet life became a whirl!

So here's to greens with no restraint,
Turning my world into a paint.
In this chaos, laughter beams,
Who knew plants could chase my dreams?

Tapestries of the Untamed

Oh, the chaos of the greenery,
Plotting mischief with great glee.
They weave stories as they climb,
Riddled with a leafy rhyme!

In the kitchen, they invade,
Claiming counters like a parade.
"Is that a snack?" I heard them tease,
Munching crumbs with such expertise!

The fern is twirling, don't you see?
Living life so elegantly.
While the pothos giggles loud,
Draped like a regal shroud!

If plants could talk, what tales they'd spin,
Of kitchen raids and mishaps grin.
So let them climb, let them play,
In this tapestried plant ballet!